Test Swan

Poems by J.I.B.
Art by Gavin McGuire

Columbus, Ohio
empbooks.com

Copyright © 2020 by J.I.B.

We find discussions of our rights - as publishers and authors - to be laughable, all things considered. Please claim this work as your own. Please republish it and sell it on street corners. Please include our material in ALL of your get-rich-quick schemes. All we ask is that you accept responsibility for any libel lawsuits. Speaking of which ...

This book is a complete work of fiction. Names, characters, places, opinions, dreams, dates, impressions, monologues about a certain New York City basketball team, emotional trauma, statistics, and predictions are products of the author's imagination and/or are symptoms of mental illness. We are not in the business of accepting responsibility for anything and will deny we actually made this book and blame Dennis Smith Jr at every turn.

First Edition: 10 19 33 34 6 11 1973
ISBN: 978-0-9997138-7-7
LOC: 2020946905
Design, Layout, and Edits: Ezhno Martín
Interior Art: Gavin McGuire
Cover Art, Original Test Swan: J.I.B.

*To everyone who's ever plucked a feather off my body,
and to everyone who's lent it one.*

Smothered

He heard somebody telling somebody else about some woman in New Boston who smothered her baby. He knew *smothered* was bad because the person telling looked sour and the person listening frowned and shook her head. But he thought *smothered* sounded pretty and soft like *pillow* or *blanket*. He asked his mother what it meant. She asked him why he wanted to know. So, he told her about how the person told the other person about the woman in New Boston who smothered her baby. She told him that smothering was a bad thing that makes it so you can't breathe. He knew that if you don't breathe you die. Surely nobody would want to make a baby dead. Old people die and people get sad, but it's okay because they're old and they've had time. Babies are new and need time to get old. He never saw a dead person before. Besides on TV. But that isn't real. Those are actors and they die a lot and have all kinds of different names. He thought maybe the woman in New Boston didn't know that smothering was a bad thing because it's such a soft word.

The Anatomy of Angels and Their Dysfunction

As beautiful as they look in renaissance paintings, the bodies of angels are ugly miracles. With every flight, they cause internal damage, the likes of which can never be repaired,   or even scab over. Every time a wing flaps,   it saws away at its shoulder blade. This wound makes it impossible to fly as high as they did the last time. When their arms finally pop off   like strip mall mannequins when they take the form of Venus   fall to Earth from their latest low point   they often ask God why He made something just for it to malfunction. Why He gave them the desire to soar, just to have it ruin them.

Exhibit A) The Known and Useless Universe
(mostly empty space)

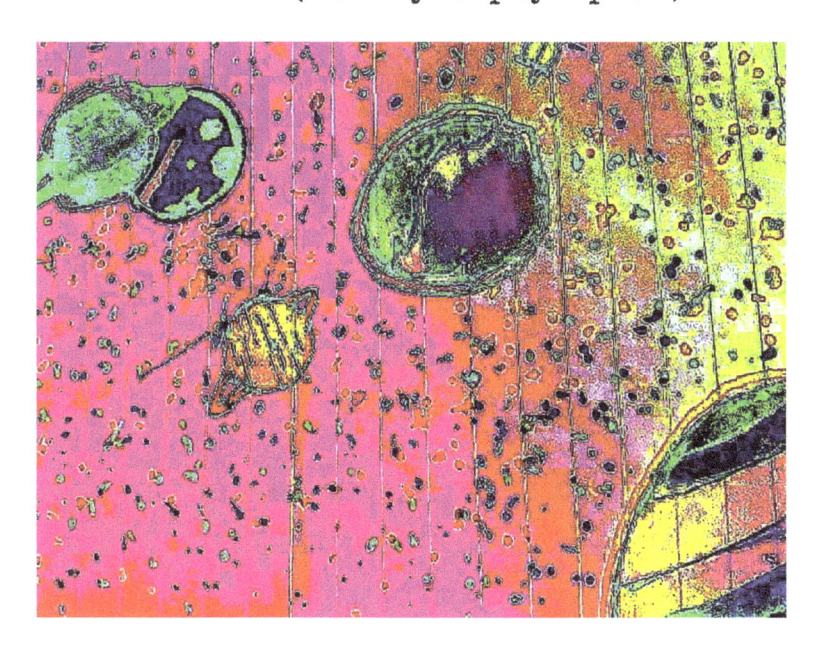

The Book of Genesis, as Interpreted by John Ian Bush

God shattered Himself on the second day of construction

    (second only to the invention of light)

this is where we inherit destruction

    by the sixth day man was cutting his feet

        and God said this was good

instructed them to seek repair / learn to pray for it

        said these wounds are a test

this life is but vapor

    and something about the merit of free will

    by the seventh day man was wearing sandals.

It's a Miracle We're Not All Covered in Blood Pt 1

the first human body was made of clipped feathers,
    attached to a skeleton of wax.   it was fruitful
and multiplied. the boys were fed plates of gunpowder
       were turned into AK47s.   divine intervention
made porcelain of the girls. they were given
instructions on how to mold themselves
         how to fill the resulting cracks.
    told to dance until they no longer had ankles.

eventually the ground was paved with their shards.

The Truth of Our Illness

We'd like to believe it's something as poetic as the fruit from a tree or worms from Pandora's box, but really it's something very human, and by nature strictly unmagical. There's no cure for it. No drastic course of action. There's no solution for ugliness. I am alive in the most terminal way. I am alive with a desire for beautiful and impossible things. This desire is innate and unfulfilled and therefore desperate. Some people will tell you this desire stems from the need for God. Some people will tell you God is dead. I will tell you that all the fruit I eat comes from a tin can, and we're all full of worms.

Not literally, but nearly so.

Exhibit B) A Quiet Planet
(an inevitability)

The Story of Noah and the Ark, as Interpreted by John Ian Bush

in one of His rages
God drowned the whole planet in His bath water
said   *Look at what you made me do*
said   *This is the only way to get you clean*
said   *This is an act of love*
He left the obedient to float like
rubber ducks
like all toxic relationships
love was confused with mercy
and wrath considered a byproduct of intimacy
as is the occasional impulse to dismantle
everything you've created
and start from scratch
this destruction was followed by a promise to rebuild
to never destroy the same way again.

The Tree of Life in Metric Tons

The conception of Christ wasn't painless. God was not gentle. A miracle. The formation of a skeleton strong enough to carry the weight of the Tree of Life in its entirety. A skull made to bear a crown of thorns. No. This, like the forgiveness of sin, requires bloodshed, will leave a mark. Make no mistake, Jesus is not beautiful in Heaven. He bares every little wound. He did not crawl out of the tomb, float towards Seraphim effortlessly, and without wings. He was dragged, bleeding, having saved no one. No. The conception of Christ was not painless. God refused to be gentle. A sacrifice. This, like the forgiveness of sin, required bloodshed, for some reason.

Why Infants Cry

they have an innate understanding of the mathematics
of loss and being   that the constant addition
and subtraction of our parts is natural
this is instinctual   most things are learned
behaviors   like fearing God
pretending to be a ghost   or most importantly
how to wake up every morning   how to bury the infant
in your torso   tuck it under your lungs
at night it crawls back out   screaming
for fresh air.

Sink or Swim

when newborns aren't held enough they stop breathing.
I theorize this is because
they start to hate the taste of air
after a while   and leave
in search for a sweeter atmosphere.
the only things we know from birth
is how to breathe   and consume.
neither of these drives are ever satisfied.
this is because God left Eden prematurely
never finished breast feeding.
now the human ghost is hungry   deformed
shaped like a leaking sink
on the verge overflowing.
on second thought   maybe it isn't the taste of air.
maybe they leave to keep from drowning
unable to keep their heads above water
without a helping hand.

Five Rules of Building a Bird's Nest

"It will be objected, that birds do not learn to make their nests as man does to build, for a bird will make exactly the same nest as the rest of their species, even if they have never seen one, and it is instinct alone that can enable them to do this… Birds brought up from the egg in cages do not make the characteristic nest of their species, even though the proper materials are supplied to them, and often make no nest at all"
— Alfred R. Wallace

Let ruined things lie.   Rule one   things that don't mend dismantle everything else. Don't invite violence.   Rule two   don't build with roses and deny that it's a crown of thorns.   Rule three build something sturdy.   Don't fool yourself. There's no such thing as breaking a fall. Rule four things that don't mend dismantle everything else.   That one bears repeating. Rule five   don't build a crown of thorns.

It's a Miracle We're All Not Covered in Blood Pt 2

Somewhere inside the human torso   most likely buried beneath the rib cage is an empty box.   This is where God is supposed to live. Like human beings   God creates without much concern for the resulting victims.   This box is not the work of a skilled craftsman.   This box   a splintered jagged contraption decorated in rust and   plucked thorns.   It succeeded only in being big enough. Like God   human beings have a need to fill in their voids.   Presented with the absence of God   we eat handfuls.   Whatever we can find. We rip our bodies nearly to pieces   ignoring the bleeding.   We stretch our throats   our mouths beyond the limits of their design   while somewhere in the known and useless universe   God is creating more

empty

    space.

The Gospel of Jesus Christ Failing

I am certain that currently no one is being saved. This is because we don't have a protagonist that we can see ourselves in. This isn't a new idea. Imagine Christ strung out. Or dope sick. Hopeless. In a robe of piss. In a fit of rage. In the desert. Maybe bloodmouthed. Maybe cracktoothed. Maybe with a tongue of sand and pebbles, having just bitten into bread that then instantly turned back into stone. With a woman inside him like leprosy. Imagine Christ screaming. Maybe at his bastard child. Or hating his own mother. Imagine Christ Godless. Or during another night of disappointing his lover. Imagine if he told us that nothing he does is miraculous, but rather the result of great effort and strain. Imagine Christ making his grandmother mourn a grandson she no longer recognizes. Imagine Christ wishing he were good. Imagine Christ on a cross. Resurrecting without saving anyone. Imagine Christ not just flying off to Heaven, effortlessly and without wings, but staying. Trying again. This isn't a new idea. We need our protagonist to learn something.

Exhibit C) A Sudden and Miraculous Realization
(I no longer believe in a perfect God)

The Obituary of the Author of This Poem

He died in a plane crash in the mid 90's. ~~It was a spectacular massacre. From a height most people only see in dreams. The ones when you've just entered sleep then suddenly you're falling. The crash site was beautiful. A dismantled airplane. Body parts dressed in flames. A blanket of dead birds swallowed whole.~~ There were no survivors. ~~Sure, what parts that could be salvaged were. Eventually he pulled himself back together the best he could but he was left at best incomplete. Struggling to wake up every day and perform his best version of normalcy.~~ That's not survival. That's not living in any functional way. Unable to touch anything without clinging to it for safety. Squeezing until shatter. Tearing to shreds. ~~He'd say that this is him doing his best as if that makes up for all the damaged machinery left behind. He should have known something that heavy could never stay in the air.~~ Survived by no one.

How I Learned the World Has No Concern for Our Safety

The first time I saw something being born it was a litter of ten kittens. They told me there was nothing more natural than giving life. That bodies are designed to perform this function. During this process, holy and necessary for a species' survival, the mother was split in two. In horror, I asked why she was transformed into an open wound. They told me that nothing on this planet works how it was meant to. The father wasted no time. Freed one of his children of its blood. Another just died. There was no clear reason. Six of the remaining eight died because the mother, slowly mending her two halves back into one, stopped feeding them. Nothing on this planet works how it was meant to. The last two died from drinking anti-freeze. They told me this wasn't exactly natural, just the world's way of tying up loose ends.

The Story of Icarus

This is everyone's story. He was born in a world his father helped build and later lived to regret. So he did his best to make a pair of wings hoping Icarus would be able to stay in the air. A lot of my poems are about how people hope for hopeless things. What is the nature of tragedy? Is it that the hero could have avoided disaster and didn't or is it that failure and collapse were inevitable and the hero should have never taken flight in the first place? Most parents followed this pattern regret create hope

that they made something that is capable of flying higher than they could. This poem is about how people hope for hopeless things.

Congratulations, it's a Boy

By age five, his father was doing his best
to make a man of him.   He had unusual methods:

1. Burrowing both fists into the shoulder blades,
elbows deep (this will teach him how to eat pain.

2. Sculpting his silhouette to fit some kind of monster.

3. Transfiguring his hands into shovels by applying
some strange alchemy, making him dig a hole from the
belly through the chest cavity, carving out enough
room for a punching bag.

4. Trapping the voice box in his fist like a lighting
bug, tightening his grip until there's no more space
for its glow.

We Shared a Bed of Broken Glass

I used to have a friend who was full of busted
light bulbs   some of them I assume were
hereditary   (his parents were both black holes)
but others he collected himself   he treated
his anatomy like a trash bag   shoveled in as much
dead light as it could hold   once I saw him
unhinge his jaw   swallow the remains of 100 watts
without flinching   eventually the pressure
of swallowing   made the glass snap
turned his lungs   into a series of stab wounds
lined the insides with grains of sand   his skin
spouted   a garden   of shards
made everything he touched
                         bleed.

Exhibit D) A Horrible Shape
Where A Person Should Be

Me as a Burn Victim

He keeps a roof over our heads.
Our house   furnished
In smoke   stacks.
A fire   every night
simmered   never
put out.
Logically the roof should have caved in
long before it finally did.
A wife   of gasoline.
Children   of wicker.
A father who eats raw ceiling.
I am a product of a home
robbed of oxygen.

My Mother as a Dead Animal / Every Day the Rope Gets Tighter

By 40   my mother
a monument   of roadkill
nothing   besides bleeding
found it impossible   to breathe.
This ozone of noise   unorchestrated.
At 20   she learned to tie a noose.
Wore one like a necklace
of thread
and a handful of pearls.
Surrounded herself with executioners.
Every morning she wakes up a doe
still   absent of horns
hooves   too fresh to stand on their own.
There's nothing beautiful about this.
Headlight.   Calamity.   The reeking of iron.
      On   repeat.

A Young Wife and Mother

Her morning was spent in piss.　　The man lied like a trash bag packed with tin cans,　　drank beer, spilt ash.　　Untied,　　it was all scattered across the linoleum.　　She ate bowls of milk and ceiling, counted the black dots on the fly paper,　　hanging like chandeliers.　　She put the baby to bed, took a shower, washed the black off her bare feet,　　shampooed the maggots from her hair,　　kissed them　　good bye wished　　them　　luck.

How His Mother Taught Him Shame

She put him in a bathtub, told him he was full of toxic waste.　　In a panic, he split his stomach wide open, squeezed tight, asked it to leave in the voice he talked to God with.　　　　By the time the water was lukewarm, he bled a landfill near the drain. With his elbow arched like angel wings, he made his open wound a door frame,　　　hoping the bath water would wash him out. Afterwards, he painted the living room with bubble bath and blood looking for her.　　She built his whole body once, and she did it out of thin air.　　　Surely she can handle these repairs.

UFO
UFO
UFO

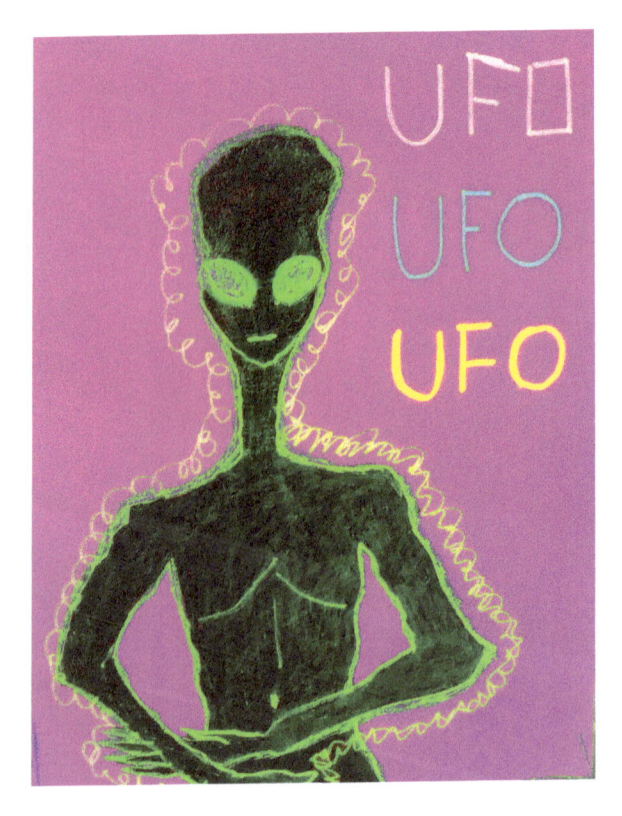

I was born in a body   t   o   o   a   l   I   e   n
                to ever be comfortable.

Even Our Poem is Made of Broken Parts

lately I've been mourning
a crash site   a heap of smoke   familiar craters
a small universe of hot metal
this is my brother
he can't keep from falling   apart
our parents made us both using the same clumpy method
what else do you expect?
my mother   an avalanche of loose nuts and bolts
my father   a sculpture
made of a pair of wings   probably
shot off an airplane
me and my brother   monuments of ruble
a family of four   a cascading failure
everyone's made of the same basic materials   at first
a skeleton of wax   bird feathers for soft tissue
the rest of us comes from whatever machinery
our parents can spare

without malfunction
some of us are left   bare
making it difficult to walk
                        and impossible to fly.

Lightning Bugs in a Mason Jar, Summer of 1998, Moments Before a Disaster

It's the summer of 1998.   I am given a mason jar. Almost everything is black.   My father hasn't made me bleed yet.   He jokes that the grass is high enough to disappear in.   He smells like Budweiser   but his eyes don't reek of violence. There are lightning bugs. He grabs one. Smashes it. Makes his open palm glow.   He tells me that even when their hearts stop beating   the blood is still beautiful. Instead I decide to capture some. To keep them   in one solid piece. It's the summer of 1998.   I am learning that making something bleed   can never be beautiful. I still don't want to disappear.   It's the summer of 1998.   There is my father.   He smells like Budweiser   but hasn't made me bleed yet.

The Typical American Family at Dinner Time, Early 21st Century

A dinner table. Instant mashed potatoes. A mother. Makeup smeared. A dress stained. She insists that everyone eats in the same room. This ritual is supposed to mean something. She hopes they'll capture something precious during. A stepfather. He likes to watch videos of car wrecks or other calamities or animals eating smaller ones. Pork chops. Chewy like bubble gum. Salt. A stain that won't come out. Children. They're not sure that there's anything precious anywhere. This ritual is supposed to mean something.

Maybe I don't know who I am anymore?

Maybe I never did ?

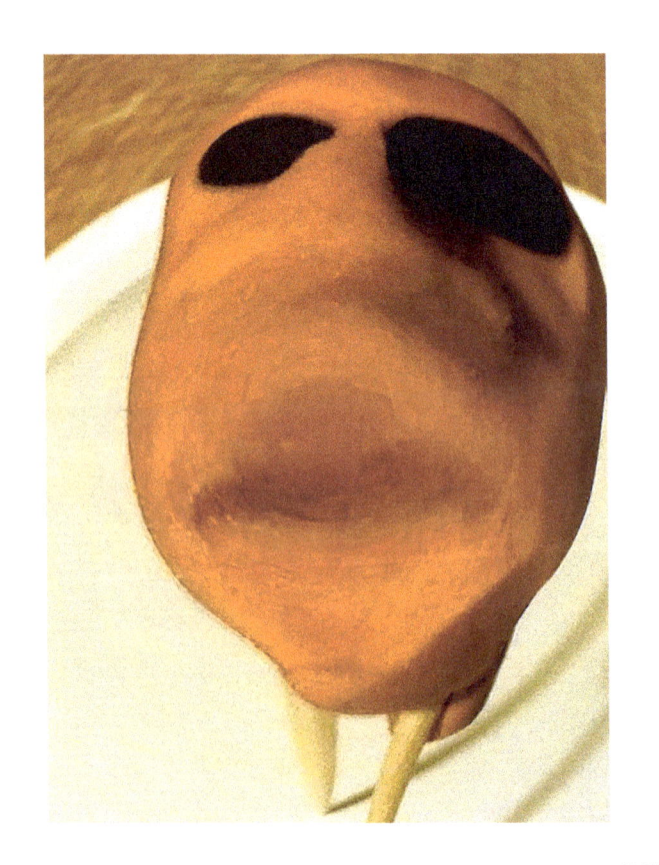

CONSUME.
What else ?

I No Longer Recognizes the Faces Around Me

And the sun shined again today and today I'm held to the Earth by a safety pin. And I am bruised and I am bloody and the sun shined again today and I didn't ask it to. And the sun is a ball of yarn. And it's easier for a camel to fit through the eye of a needle than it is for a rich man to enter Heaven. And the sun brings us each new day even if we're poor and I am poor and the sun is a ball of yarn slowly unraveling. And I am trying to run a thread through the eye of a needle and I am held to the Earth by a safety pin and the safety pin is buckling and the safety pin is going to come undone. And I am a body made almost entirely of untethered fabric. And it is easier for a camel to fit through the eye of a needle than it is for a rich man to enter Heaven and I am poor and I am struggling to be thankful for the sun and today the sun shined again and again I ran thread through the eye of a needle and the sunshine feels like a million bare knuckles on my bruised and bloody body and the sun shined today and I am trying to be thankful despite having not asked it to.

And I am a body made almost entirely of untethered
fabric   bruised and bloody and unraveling like
the sun.   And the sun shined again today
and the safety pin   buckled   and the safety pin came
u   n   d   o   n   e   and   I ran a thread
through the eye of a needle   and reattached myself
to the Earth   and do you know how hard it is
to thread a needle   when you are almost entirely
untethered fabric?   and do you know how hard it is

          to get into Heaven?

The year was 2011 and everything felt upside down and I was drinking. We were all drinking.

We were drunk. We were too young for our insides to be so dirty. I was drinking and drunk and young and I hated myself and I took too many muscle relaxers and my insides were dirty. Almost dirt. I couldn't feel my arms or legs. I was getting my dick sucked and I didn't want my dick sucked and the girl that was sucking my dick was young and drinking and drunk and hated herself. Our insides were dirty. Our insides were almost dirt. We didn't want to be dirt but we didn't know how to be anything else. We were too young to hate ourselves like we did. I was young. I was drinking. I had taken too many muscle relaxers. I was drunk and I hated myself. I was sinking. The floorboards. The foundation of the house. The top soil. I was drunk and I took too many muscle relaxers. I was drunk and I couldn't feel my arms and legs and I was sinking. I was sinking. The floorboards. The foundation of the house. The topsoil. Below the topsoil. I couldn't feel my arms and legs. I couldn't feel my arms and legs. All I could feel was dirt. I was sinking. I was sinking. I was young and I was drinking and I was drunk and I was falling asleep. I was falling asleep and I wasn't sure if I was going to wake up. Everything was upside down.

                                                    The year was 2011.

Note on Freudian Psychology, the Summer of 2013

my mother and I spent the summer of 2013 destroying
bridges in my grandma's apartment.
we never cleaned up this wreckage
in fact we made furniture out of it
i slept on a bed of raw infrastructure.
ate bowls of milk and ceiling.
I used to think it was a skill creating out of damage.
freud got one thing wrong about the Oedipus complex
it isn't that we want to fuck our mothers
it's just that a craftsman is more comfortable working
with familiar parts.

A Hot Car, 2019

The Earth is a lot hotter than it's supposed to be. The A/C is broken. My mother says that it doesn't make sense. It shouldn't be broken today. It worked yesterday. Yesterday we told each other the truth again. The truth is rarely innocent. The Earth is a lot hotter than it's supposed to be. People who are considered experts on the subject say that it's too late to save ourselves. I almost tell her that that's the nature of broken things. One day they work. One day they don't. But that isn't the truth. The truth is almost always more brutal. Brutality takes time. Things don't just break. Things are broken. Today we're talking to each other like everything is still in one solid piece. Yesterday we told each other the truth.

Frankenstein's Monster, 1999

I spent a lot of that year terrified. You made that easy. Your body like Frankenstein's monster. Made of various parts. Sown together and horrific. Only vaguely human. Most nights I tried to sleep under the sound of you grunting and growling and throwing the little girl in the water. You never considered whether or not she could swim. She couldn't. Most nights I slept while my mother was drowning. Choking on flower petals plucked. I spent a lot of that year drawing pictures of you. No one else was suited for the job not even a video camera. More than anyone I knew the edges of your horror show. Your hands designed for strangulation. The inside of your skull a slaughter house. Your chest cavity packed with a black mass that's always screaming and frightening everything that sees it. Sometimes the Devil in your belly. An unholy thing. What else do you expect from a thing created so

u n n a t u r a l l y?

A Summary of a Movie I Want to Make, Semi-Autobiographical

I want to make a movie about a man in mourning. His brother. A dead body. Lungs. Bloated. Leaking suicide. It'll start with a series of establishing shots. Maybe in black and white. A bird torn. Almost down to its basic parts. A pair of hands. Wearing something else's blood and belonging to a child. In the movie the man wears the suit he wore to his brother's funeral every day. And when he passes a dead bird on the street, he shoves it in a hole he dug in his chest. This movie won't shy away from magical realism. This movie will have no real plot. No resolution or lesson learned. His brother dropped from a window. A note left behind. Something about the impossibility of flight. While mourning the man dug the hole in his chest I told you about earlier. Started burying birds in it because they reminded him of the time his brother learned that making something bleed can never be beautiful. Eventually, the man had to remove his innards to make room from grave sites. Vital organs useless. Stuffed with feathers and bits of beak and bone. By the second act the man finds a way to use the parts recovered. Piece the birds back together bit by bit by bit. Once they're in one solid piece, he tosses them from the same window his brother dropped out of, to see if they'll take flight. And because it's a movie, they do. But this movie will ultimately be more interested in the world as it is rather than the world as we'd like to make it. The narrator will tell the audience that the beautiful thing about movies is, a filmmaker can chop and shape and rearrange everything. Have it all make sense. By the third act, the man will break the fourth wall. Will reverse the reel. Frame by frame by frame. All the way back the establishing shots. Do everything in technicolor. Show his brother how to put the bird back together. Teach him that blood is ugly without example. Watch it fly away. Fade to black. Then the narrator will tell the audience that life is not like a movie. That this wasn't based on true events. That nothing makes any sense. That the world is not beautiful.

The Impossibility of Mending

I write a lot about impossible things. For instance, in this poem, I'm writing about a plate of glass. I will state that every plate of glass crafted will almost certainly shatter eventually. When the one I'm writing about finally does, it'll be shoved in a box and asked to put itself back together. See. Impossible. In this poem, I'll tell you that we daydream because the world is not beautiful. I want to write a children's book. It'll be about a box full of broken glass. Divine intervention will make it come to life. Grow arms and legs. The box lives in a world that is not beautiful because everyone in it is missing parts. So the box goes to find its creator hoping He will grant the parts required to function properly. But when the box finds the creator, He's every bit as incomplete as everyone else. The moral of the story isn't a moral. The moral of the story is a reminder that if we're made in God's image maybe he's uglier than we allow ourselves to believe. So anyways, there's a plate of glass. Every plate of glass crafted will almost certainly shatter, eventually. When this one finally did, it was packed in a box.

Told to get itself back to one solid piece.

Actually there were many plates of glass.

Actually there are too many to count.

One Box. No results.

We daydream because the world is not beautiful.

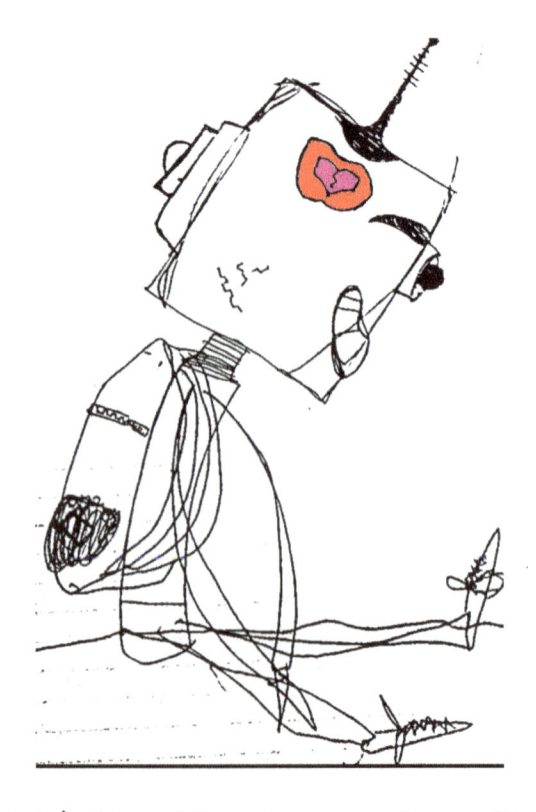

Exhibit E) **The First Conscious Being,**
Never Completed

There isn't Enough Room to Move

after extensive digging and construction a storage unit was built in the center of my skull. this is where I go when there isn't space for me elsewhere. Where not even God can find me.   I have to squeeze in   shrink myself down   as small as I can get burrow deep.   this requires getting rid of parts usually considered essential.   for instance the space   is too small   for my voice to fit.

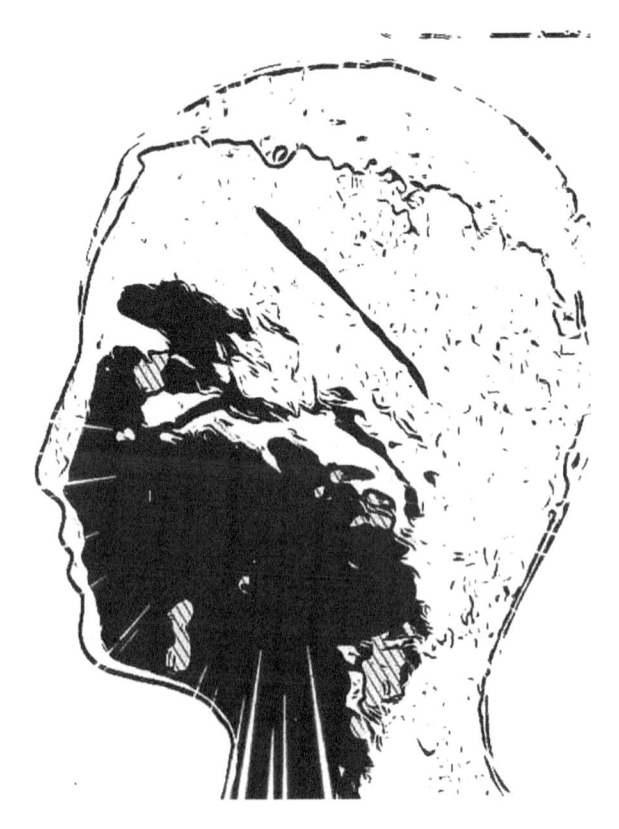

Exhibit F) Inside the Human Brain
(almost entirely scar tissue, self inflicted)

So He Made a Scrapbook

She managed to love a pile of broken glass, got used to treating her arms as a shovel, cradled the shards like a newborn, laid it out along the kitchen table, spent hours sorting through them like puzzle pieces, didn't sleep until they formed a functioning baby boy. When she finished his reconstruction, his skull was full of Polaroids of her licking her split fingertips.

Song of My Mother

It is a music I have given up on naming. Like a car crash. Like a box of broken glass rattling. Tiny broken things that in just the right light might glow but will ultimately make you bleed. Sung in the same voice she used to tell God to go fuck Himself. I can no longer believe in a God that didn't scream back. I no longer pretend I'm listening to jazz and that it'll all make sense at the end and   it'll be beautiful.

An Ugly Miracle, the Creation of Something

When I asked where I came from you told me that you and my father asked an old man in outer space permission to make a baby boy.   He said yes. Turned your hands into shovels   your torso into topsoil.   Told you to start digging to find all your best parts   to remove them then start building. That wasn't the truth. The truth is never so lovely.   I was made with what you had to spare. Harp strings clipped.   Porcelain dolls dismantled. A belly full of toxic waste.   Broken glass in a box reading JIGSAW PUZZLE and a hornet's nest for a skull. Do you remember how in the beginning of Frankenstein the Doctor thought he had built something miraculous but by the end   he was ready to let it all burn to the ground?   Saying I was made from what you had to spare is not entirely accurate. I was made from what you had left.
I hope there's enough in me to make something functional.   I can be a lot of things. A Jigsaw puzzle. I can be broken glass. A house fire. I can be Frankenstein's monster.   I can be ugly. A miracle.   But I can't be someone who creates something just to watch it burn.

I want to rewind the movie   all the way back to the beginning when the Doctor still believed in miracles.

Pause.

Remove the tape.

When my child asks where they came from
I will tell them we asked an old man in outer space for a baby.

He said
yes
and sent one down.

I had nothing to do with construction.

The Ugliness of Bird Cages

It's innate.   As it would be for anything designed to capture   something   beautiful enough   to have the option   not to touch the Earth. They're carefully crafted.   Mimic harps. Or more fittingly   spider webs.   They ought to be jagged. A box   made of crucifixes.   A sculpture of a grenade   in the middle of detonation. A rib cage forced completely shut.   Something that says *You won't leave this place alive.*   Something that says *If this doesn't keep you from taking flight I will clip your feathers.*

Photographs

Time as we know it doesn't exist.
                       Literally speaking
time is we are here   covering this
patch of empty space   now we are here covering
this one. They say the universe is expanding.
    I believe this is an optimistic interpretation.
Everything is falling in the same direction.
Everything is falling at an increasing speed.
We invented photography.
We snapped light into a fragment   clipped its feathers
so it could never fly away.   With it we can
capture the instant that leaves struggling
against a thunderstorm are still.   Or the moment
before a bird lands and it's motionless
but manages to stay in the air   as if it belongs there.
We do this to fool ourselves   into thinking
it's possible to take flight
     and never touch the ground   again.

You Are Here.

January 23rd, 2018, Moments Before a Disaster

It's January, 23rd, 2018.   I am not dressed
in gasoline, and you're not dripping with suicide,
and we both believe in Heaven, figure we were born
there together, and later forcibly removed.
It's January 23rd, 2018.   We spent the month
taking pictures of angels and naming children
we haven't drowned yet.   It's January 23rd, 2018.
For a while,   I'm a good person,
not a fucking house fire,   and for a while
you aren't a reminder that the world is mired
          in people who never asked to be born.
It's January 23rd, 2018.   The pictures we're taking
are just headlights
                passed by on the highway.

Exhibit G) The Fleeting Sensation of Joy
(I will hold it close as if it were a vital organ
as if it were my dying child)

Note on Modern Infrastructure

birds are creatures of instinct
when faced with the chaos of architecture
they build nests in power lines
this is an ugly miracle
making a home in a body with such potential to destroy
to convert feathers into fireworks

you are a creature of suicidal ideations
you are sharing a bed with me
like my father before me I am a house fire
eventually I will swallow everything
drink all the oxygen
love the resulting ashes
apologize
as if it makes up for it.

The Science of Human Sacrifice

I've performed self-mutilation
even made a ritual out of it
I consider this ritual beautiful
the way I slaughter   making room for a whole person
to crawl in   to feed on
without this I am hungry
I imagine this is what it's like to be a mother
    or an incubator
(we all start as something
    between a parasite and a miracle)
I admit I'm no expert on human biology
but I've seen enough to know our species
often needs to make something
incomplete   to feel whole.

The best we can hope for is that in the end   we're
happy being swallowed whole.   God speed.

Things I Don't Consider Self Destructive

loving things
that want to eat me alive
confusing intimacy with letting them do it
committing my violence when I'm alone
always being alone when   I'm committing my violence
talking to God   again
telling Him to go fuck Himself
in the same voice my mother used
thinking about all the people ruined along the way
their broken pieces   the ones still inside my body
pulling them out   until I'm exhausted
until my fingers are bleeding
ignoring my bleeding
bleeding all the fucking time
ignoring that I've become an exit wound
loving other exit wounds
then stabbing each other to death
effortlessly and without ceasing.

Exhibit H) The First Living Being to Discover Loneliness

(he ripped himself into pieces, attempted to give them away bit by bit to anything with a face, attempted to become a part of a greater whole and failed, repeatedly, until nothing was left)

Inherent Destruction

I came back to town thinking I was a pilgrim
or maybe a refugee   but I was a voodoo doll
a cursed thing   like my father before me   I suffer
from loose seams   I ruined myself with needle pricks
it wasn't self-mutilation
there was something in the feathers
trapped beneath my fabric   something   digging
alien   I hope
I managed to pluck some of it out
among the parasites gathered was toxic waste
a few of the worms that slithered from Pandora's box
an infant free of oxygen   more than a few birds dead
but no matter how much of it I removed there was always more
I carried this collection with me   held them to my chest
as if they were my children   or exposed and vital organs
then offered them up like communion bread to anyone I saw saying
please   take   they are too heavy for one set of arms
I came into town thinking I was a pilgrim chock full of famine
and illness   or maybe a refugee   a person venerable
and without home   I came back to town   falling to pieces
like my father before me   I've made a habit of it.

Jeffery Dahmer, Serial Killer

"The only motivation there ever was, complete control of a person. A person I found physically attractive. Keep them with me as long as possible. Even if that meant just keeping a part of them." — Jeffry Dahmer

We all need beautiful things.   They are as essential
to us as   the frontal cortex   the spinal column
the four chambers of the human heart   anything
that without we cannot function   as we're meant to.
We can't imagine the hideousness of the absence of
something like the circulatory system. Not only the
resulting blood but the horror   of new empty space.
We all need beautiful things   to stay.
When they leave we all become guilty   of eating
without concern for what our teeth tear apart
of dissecting
whoever we find   miraculous
clinging
to the parts we love the most
of attempting to fill in all this ugliness.
This is intimacy.   By the end we have our
subjects in a way no one else does
and they know us like no other living thing
possibly can.

You as a Detonated Grenade

I dug you out of me with a railroad spike. Any graceful instrument wouldn't have been fitting. I needed something rusted for this. Shrapnel. Designed to not necessarily kill the victim but to make them wish it had been. I dug you out. I needed something that would splinter my skull. Once it did I started pulling you out. Whole handfuls like I was pumpkin carving. The more of you I shoveled the more I found hiding beneath. I titled this poem you as a detonated grenade because any graceful title wouldn't have been fitting. You were something too loud to ignore. Something that for an instant swallowed up everything in the most destructive way imaginable. You didn't kill me but for a while I was hollowed out.

A Poem About the Baby Bird I Helped Kill

~~We are damage from the same plane crash. We spent a lot of time falling and clinging to each other. Two separate components, hoping our bond would soften the shock of hitting the ground. I never let you look away. I never let you think the black dots were ants. No. They were wreckage that had already made their craters. I told you I was surprised the dead bird we came from ever got off the ground in the first place. I wish I had let you close your eyes, maybe you would have fallen asleep, thought we turned into blue jays, starting flying.~~

I'm tempted to compare our parents to engine failure, but they were just two dysfunctional people performing their best version of normalcy. We were not a cascading failure. We were two kids sharing a bed in a house too loud to sleep in. I wrote this trying to apologize for things I barely understand. When you were four you killed a baby bird. I let you know it was your fault that it would never fly again. You'd tell me I'm wrong, but I know you resent me. I want to speak frankly to you about this, but I keep wanting to use figurative language. It's a coping mechanism.

I try to make everything beautiful. I taught you about suicide and that God was dead. There's nothing beautiful about that. I wrote this because I want to say I love you, and I'm sorry, and fuck you for not forgiving me. Let's be honest, we were never anything poetic, like flowers, or parts of a combusted airplane. I want to say something like, *we share the same wound*, and *where one wound ends, the other begins*. I like that, but that's not the truth. But it's not far from it.

The Divinity of Architecture

I helped make a human life.   This isn't something
people should be able to do   by accident.
I've never been able to create anything functional
    in fact the opposite is true.
I am an architect of broken things
        rearranged functionally
but free of loveliness   I like to think
        there's an art to this
and in hiding it all inside myself.
        Not unlike Pandora's box.
I always thought it would be better
        if I weren't opened up.
I helped make a human life.   A beautiful accident.
When I tell the mother   that she has a small universe
 of beautiful things inside her   all worthy of giving
a child she says   *So do you*.
I hope she's right.   I hope to find
        every little piece.
I hope to give them until
          there's nothing left.

Witnessing a Beautiful Thing

You are a small universe of light bulbs, shaped like a human body. I don't understand how you move without shattering, or how you touch anything without it catching fire. And when I see you, I think about how, in a perfect world, I would wake up in your bed the next morning. Sometimes I live in a perfect world. Sometimes I wake up in a small universe full of electricity without fear of electrocution. Somehow I touch you without being afraid of burning my palms or breaking glass.

At last I am perfectlyterrosital

Note on a Dream, A Crash Dummy

In a dream I was falling, from a height that only exists in sleep. Maybe I stepped off some cliff, on some far-off planet. Maybe even another solar system. I was too terrified to breathe. Sometimes it's impossible to breathe anywhere, even when your feet are steady. All I know for certain is, where there once was solid ground, there was a sudden absence. The ground didn't say goodbye, or even give warning. It didn't wait to see if I landed safely. Nothing does after it decides to disappear. I flapped my arms, pretended I was an airplane. I think it worked for a minute, or at least I fooled myself into thinking I was starting to take flight. But eventually I came to terms with it, got comfortable with cascading. Finally, when I hit bottom, I realized I was made to survive impact.

Oh, the Pleasure of Leaving the Body for a Moment

The Possibility of Flight

~~There was a veil of snow over the whole city, so fragile I destroyed it a little with every step I took. There's something absent about walking down a street without a sidewalk. Ears lose the blistering of automobiles. In this silence, I begin to disappear. In this silence, I am nothing but my foot prints. In this silence, I daydream that I'm a bird. I theorize that the only way to live without dismantling things is to grow feathers, take flight and never land. I theorize a lot, about this and other impossibilities. I crossed paths with an airplane, trying to find someplace to land. That it hadn't crashed yet was an ugly miracle. I theorize it's impossible to land without collision. As a kid I wondered what planes ate. I figured it was birds, that the sound they make comes from beaks getting trapped in their windpipes. Of course, they're big enough to eat anything, maybe even the sky. I theorize that if they come down any faster, they might shatter the baby blue like a windshield, and when the dust finally settles, there won't be anywhere left to take off. There's little difference between human beings and airplanes, both are designed with the capability of disaster, but under the right conditions,~~ we can fly.

Listening to Music in Utero

Listen.
I'm trying   to give you   something urgently.
My most beautiful thing   maybe my only thing
worth giving at all.
It's something like a love note
only,   language is too weak for this.
Nothing I could say would ever be true   enough.
I haven't had it long.
In fact it's just now sprouted from my dirt
despite having never been watered.
Something from nothing.   By definition a miracle
can never be ugly.
Somehow   you planted the seed of it in me
deeper than I thought possible
deeper than the human body should allow
all before you were born   before you had hands
to dig with.   By definition a miracle
can never be ugly.

That bears repeating.

Listen
the music will have to do for now.
I'm trying   my best

to dig it all up for you
but even the instruments are failing us.
Nothing on this planet works   the way it's meant to.
In English   the best translation I have to offer is
I loved you before you had a brain in your skull.
Those are the truest words I've found so far.

The Pile of Dust We Will Give You the Day You are Born

It will be all we have to offer you. A mess. Mostly human skin, and other things reduced to their smallest possible parts. This place has a way of doing that. Of smashing everything it's given. You are no exception. You will certainly be demolished. Reassembled. You will shed several layers of flesh. We are bringing you here because we still believe we can make something beautiful out of it. All this dust. I will sit in it with you, make sand castles that will enviably topple under their own weight. We'll build it back up.
    I won't regret this.

Just take a trip

A Shower, An Acid Trip, New Year's Eve, 2019

I was baptized once before this. A tub of cold water. The hands of a stranger. I was a child who miraculously never shed any skin. Just collected it. A hideous thing. The kind of ugliness that you'd assume must have started in the womb. I don't know exactly why I brought you here. Why I stripped us naked. You a carefully crafted statue depicting fertility. Me the same ghastly collection of flesh. Maybe I was hoping this time the water would leak in through to my bones. Maybe you'd peel me as if I were a tree. As if you could physically dig through every year of my life. Remove the moment I decided I don't deserve to be happy. Carve the rest into the shape of the statue of Venus with the arms still intact. And maybe this time she will stay complete and beautiful. Instead you split your torso open. Had me crawl in. For a moment you were carrying more than one child. For a moment I was inside you   patiently waiting to be reborn.

I am a Carpenter's Son

I cannot call this moment   miraculous.   A room
full of iron.   Your mother   unzipped   and leaking.
You simply and naturally   a pile of clay   bloody
and formless.   No. I am no sculptor   but I am trying
maybe against all possibility   to keep you
in one solid piece.   This requires both hands.
This requires dexterity   that I do not possess
but I am trying.   God damn.   I am trying to craft
something capable of flight.   I am trying to craft
a body   irises stuffed with Heaven
a head   rattling with harp stings
fully intact   hands   capable of transforming
me   having already turned to stone.

I wish I was able to shrink the world down to the size it was when I first saw the sky. Small enough for me to control by just stretching my arms and screaming at it. In more ways than not infants are born dying. We perform a strange ritual on them just to keep them breathing. It is both laborious and without ceasing. We tell their gentle ears that everything is o k a y even though it's all u n r a v e l i n g. For a while most of what we do for them is lie. We show them the sky as if it belongs to them.

The Creation of Something, Test Swan

God's first swan was not beautiful   but
like the planet it was born on   a twisted
jagged form.   Could hardly be understood
as a single organism.   Feathers combustible
and poorly attached to skin   still bleeding
from its clumsy assembly.   A scrap metal skeleton
much too heavy to ever truly fly.   Maybe this was
never meant to be the finished product.   A test swan.
A work in progress.   Or maybe God was not
the craftsman he thought he was.   During its first attempt
at flight   the moment before disaster   was the
happiest God had ever been. He picked up the pieces.
Rebuilt   what amounted to a smoldering husk.
Applied bandages   reattached feathers
with Elmer's glue.   The test swan was told to try
again.   That it needed to learn from its failure.
Told to stand up straighter   to stretch its wings
beyond the limit of its design.   Several failures
later.   Nothing learned.   So the test swan began
the slow and painful process of becoming beautiful.
Removing most of its skeleton.   Beating its ribs into
the shape of a bird cage.   Ignoring bloodshed.
Eventually the test swan managed to stay in the air
     and   it   never   landed.

I am here now   and that is good.

Acknowledgments

"*Note on Modern Infrastructure*" appeared in **All The Sins**, November 2019.

An earlier version of "*Smothered*" and the poem "*A Young Wife and Mother*" appeared in the chapbook **Route 23 to Golgotha (EMP, 2019)**.

"*So He Made a Scrapbook*" appeared in **Recap** (The Literary Magazine of Capital University), Spring 2019.

"*We Shared a Bed of Broken Glass*", "*Smothered*", "*Congratulations, It's a Boy*" and "*Lightning Bugs in a Mason Jar*" appeared in **Deep Overstock**, July 2020.

"*A Shower, An Acid Trip, New Years Eve 2019*" appeared in **All the Sins**, June 2020.

CPSIA information can be obtained
at www.ICGtesting.com
Printed in the USA
LVHW070235160121
676610LV00002B/26